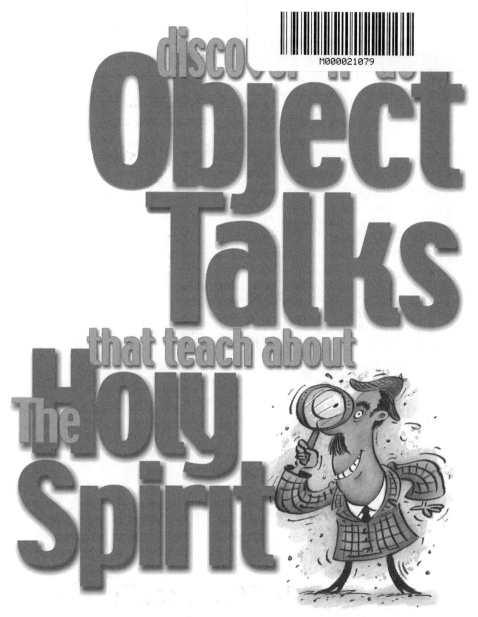

discover it fast

Object Talks

that teach about

The Holy Spirit

SUSAN L. LINGO

Standard®
PUBLISHING
Bringing The Word to Life

Cincinnati, Ohio

DEDICATION

But seek first his kingdom and his righteousness,
and all these things will be given to you as well.
Matthew 6:33

Discover-n-Do Object Talks That Teach About the Holy Spirit
Copyright © 2002 by Susan L. Lingo

Published by Standard Publishing, Cincinnati, Ohio
www.standardpub.com

Credits
Produced by Susan L. Lingo, Bright Ideas Books™
Illustrated by Paula Becker
Cover design by Joel Armstrong

09 08 07   5 4
ISBN-13: 978-0-7847-1373-0
ISBN-10: 0-7847-1373-1

CONTENTS

INTRODUCTION

What would you do if you saw ...
   ✔ **Three scarves become one?**
   ✔ **A tiny purse with a 2-foot rod inside?**
   ✔ **Bubbling water from your fingertips?**
   ✔ **An amazing X-ray tube?**

What would you do? Why, you'd probably race to discover how it was done! And while you were making those exciting discoveries, you'd discover some amazing Bible truths, too! That's what *Discover-n-Do Object Talks That Teach About the Holy Spirit* is all about. These object talks are different from other ho-hum chats. Here are twenty-three unique, eye-popping presentations and mighty messages that drive home important Bible truths and God's Word. Just think how excited your kids will be to see through their hands with an X-ray tube as they discover the importance of discernment or how tickled they'll be seeing a 2-foot wooden rod being pulled from a coin purse as they learn that the Holy Spirit is with us forever. These are eye-popping object talks that inspire heart-warming responses to God's Word! But wait ... are these cool demonstrations, memorable messages, and slick tricks easy enough for any teacher to prepare and present? Yes! Simple supplies and clear-cut directions are provided and guarantee to turn any teacher into an object-talk pro while grabbing kids' attention in unique and memorable ways!

Each object talk opens with a case to be solved, such as "Is there really power in prayer?" Then, following every slick trick or powerful presentation, kids will collect clues to solve the case by reading the Bible and discovering the answers God gives us through his Word. Brief discussions and fun extra-time activities round out the object talks and provide meaningful, memorable fun for kids of all ages!

So what are you waiting for? Grab your sleuth's hat and magnifying glass, put on your gumshoes, and lead kids in discovering powerful truths about the Holy Spirit in God's Word with *Discover-n-Do Object Talks That Teach About Holy Spirit!* Be sure to look for the other Discover-n-Do Object Talks books in the series: *Discover-n-Do Object Talks That Teach About God and Discover-n-Do Object Talks That Teach About Jesus!*

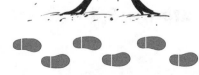

⌕ JESUS' GREAT GIFT

John 14:16, 17, 26; 15:26; 20:22; Acts 2:1-4

The Case: *Why did Jesus send us the Holy Spirit?*

Simple Supplies: You'll need a Bible, paper lunch sacks, scissors, paper punch, glue, confetti, and picture of a gift. If you plan on doing the extra-time activity, you'll need paper plates, fishing line, markers, tape, and red, orange, and yellow tissue paper.

Before class, prepare and practice this awesome trick. (You'll need to prepare two double sacks: one for practice and one for the actual demonstration.) In this demonstration, you place a picture of a festive gift in a paper sack, blow up the sack and pop it, and whoosh—colorful confetti "explodes" from the sack and the paper gift is nowhere to be seen! To make the secret sacks, begin by cutting off the top 2 inches of one sack. Now use a paper punch to punch about ten holes in the bottom of that sack. Into the second sack, place a layer of confetti. Slide the perforated sack into the bag above the confetti and glue the edges of the short sack to the inside edges of the outer sack. Draw a colorful gift on white paper and cut out the gift. During the object talk, you'll place the paper gift into the sack. (The audience will think there is only one sack, but you'll really be placing the gift into the smaller sack!) Blow the sack up until it bursts. (As you blow, air will be forced through the holes of the inner sack into the outer sack. Since there's no pressure on the inner sack, only the outer one will burst and rain out confetti.) As the confetti showers down, quickly crumple the rest of the sack containing the paper gift and set it aside. (Hint: If the outer bag fails to burst after blowing into it, simply pop the sack with your hands—remember your school lunchroom? Those sacks made some noisy pops, didn't they?)

Discover 'n Do!

Gather kids and hold the bag with the hidden confetti. Hold the paper gift in your other hand. Ask kids to briefly tell about wonderful gifts they've received and why those gifts were so special. Then hold up the paper gift and say: **Gifts are so exciting, aren't they? And when we receive special gifts, we can be sure they are given with great love. Jesus promised his followers a very special gift to be given after he was risen to heaven. But when Jesus ascended to his heavenly Father, his followers wondered where the special gift was. It was almost as if his promise had disappeared into the clouds as Jesus had.** (Place the paper gift inside the sack.) **Several days later, Jesus' followers were in a place waiting for Jesus' special gift when they heard sounds like the great blowing of wind. Then all at once** (blow the sack up to pop it, or use your hands to explode the sack, then hide the remaining sack quickly) **pow! The gift of the Holy Spirit burst**

into their lives and hearts bringing joy, love, and God's power! And just as the Holy Spirit burst into his followers' lives, Jesus' perfect gift bursts into ours, too!

But why did Jesus want to give us this special gift? Why did Jesus send us the gift of the Holy Spirit? Let's see if we can solve the case with a little detective work and the Bible!

Collect the Clues!

Have volunteers read aloud Acts 2:1-4; John 14:16, 17, 26; and 15:26. Then ask:

✔ Why did Jesus send us the gift of the Holy Spirit?

✔ Why did Jesus think we needed the help and power of the Spirit?

✔ In what ways is the Holy Spirit like having Jesus right here with us all the time?

Say: **Because Jesus loved us so greatly, he wanted to give us a gift that was filled with love, joy, help, and heavenly power. The Holy Spirit is all these things and more and was sent by Jesus to be our friend, counselor, and teacher. What a powerful, perfect gift! And we can use and enjoy the wonderful gift of the Holy Spirit every day of our lives.** Close by saying: **Good for you—you've solved the clues! Jesus sent us the gift of the Holy Spirit to love and guide us and stay beside us. The case is closed!**

If there's time, let kids make Holy Spirit spirals. For each spiral, draw a tiny dot in the center of a paper plate. Cut the plate in a round-n-round spiral fashion beginning at one edge and continuing until you come to the dot. Then write: ***Jesus said, "Receive the Holy Spirit"*** from John 20:22 along the spiral, beginning with the first word beside the dot and continuing around the spiral. Tape torn tissue-paper flames to the edges of the spiral, then finish by taping an 18-inch length of fishing line to the dot. Tell kids to hang their Holy Spirit spirals near a breezy window as they remember how Jesus sent the Spirit to love and guide us.

ERRIFIC TRIO

Matthew 16:16; John 8:41; 14:16; 2 Corinthians 13:14

The Case: *What is the "Trinity"?*

Simple Supplies: You'll need a Bible, newsprint, a marker and tape, and two small bananas (one to practice with and one for the object talk). If you plan on doing the extra-time activity, you'll need maraschino cherries, drained pineapple chunks, paper plates, napkins, and a small banana for each child.

Before class, try this simple, but simply awesome, trick to illustrate the 3-in-1, 1-in-3 concept of the Trinity. Peel a banana halfway, then slowly slide your index

finger down into the center of the banana top. As your finger slides further into the banana, the banana will split itself into three equal sections. (Neat, isn't it?) You'll use this demonstration to show kids how the Trinity is made of three persons yet is still one God. For the extra-time activity, kids will be making yummy fruit salads to reinforce the Trinity as a 3-in-1, 1-in-3 concept. Purchase a small banana for each child to try this trick and add to his salad. (Hint: Choose bananas that are as straight as possible and are firm—not mushy.) Tape a large sheet of newsprint to the wall.

Discover 'n Do!

Gather kids and hold up the banana. Ask kids to tell how bananas are usually sliced, then ask kids if they think it's possible to slice the banana into three pieces by only touching the banana once with one finger. After several moments of discussion, peel half the banana, then position your finger at the top center of the banana. Say: **I will now show you how to slice a banana into three parts with one motion!** Push your finger into the banana to make three sections, then show kids the resulting slices. Say: **Wow! It is possible to make one part into three parts and back into one again!** Slide your hand up the banana to make the three parts stick together as one piece again.

Say: **This neat little banana trick can help us understand how God, Jesus, and the Holy Spirit are related in what we call the "Trinity." But what is the Trinity, and how does the Holy Spirit fit into God's power team? Let's see if we can solve the case with a little detective work and the Bible!**

Collect the Clues!

Gather kids by the large sheet of newsprint taped to the wall and have a marker ready. Invite a volunteer to use the marker to divide the paper into three sections. Say: **Just as this one sheet of paper has three parts, God's power team has three members.** Have kids read aloud John 8:41b ("The only Father we have is God himself"). Then write the name "God" at the top of the first section and write the word "Father" below it. Say: **The first person in the Trinity is God the Father. God created the heavens and the earth and people to live here. We know that God is our heavenly Father and is all-powerful and wise! Who is the next person in the Trinity? Let's find out.**

Have kids read aloud Matthew 16:16 ("Simon Peter answered, 'You are the Christ, the Son of the living God.'") Then write the name "Jesus" at the top of the second section and the word "Son" below it. Say: **The next person in the Trinity is Jesus, God's Son. We know that God sent his Son to love us and to offer us eternal forgiveness and life through**

his death and resurrection. So far we have God the Father and Jesus the Son. Who is the third person in the Trinity? Let's see what we can discover!

Have kids read aloud John 14:16, 17a ("And I will ask the Father, and he will give you another Counselor to be with you forever—the Spirit of truth.") Then write the name "Holy Spirit" at the top of the third section and write the word "Counselor" below it. Say: **The third person in the Trinity is the Holy Spirit, God's Spirit and the helper and friend Jesus promised to send. We know that Jesus sent the Holy Spirit to love and guide us and to help us accomplish God's will on earth. In the Trinity, then, there is God the Father, Jesus the Son, and the Holy Spirit, our counselor and helper. What a terrific trio of power and perfect love!** Ask:

✔ **How does knowing we have the power and love of the Trinity give us a "triple treat" in our lives?**

✔ **In what ways does each person in the Trinity help us? teach us?**

Say: **The Trinity is God's heavenly power team: three persons in one, and one in three—and unlike our banana, they can never be separated. And each person in the Trinity is divine, eternal, and all-powerful. I'm so glad I have a heavenly, triple power team I can have faith in, aren't you?** Read 2 Corinthians 13:14, then close by saying: **Good for you—you've solved the clues! The Trinity consists of God the Father, Jesus the Son, and the Holy Spirit, who is our teacher and friend. The case is closed!**

If there's time, invite kids to try the neat trick of splitting bananas into three equal sections. Then place the bananas on paper plates and let each child add a cherry and chunk of pineapple to make Trinity Treat Fruit Salad. Before kids nibble their delights, point out how the three fruits are in one salad and how God's power team is three persons in one. Offer a prayer thanking God for each person in the Trinity.

WHATTA NAME!

Isaiah 11:2; Matthew 3:16; John 14:17; 1 Peter 4:14

The Case: *What are names for the Holy Spirit?*

Simple Supplies: You'll need a Bible, an empty cereal box, poster board, scissors, tape, a marker, and eight slips of paper. If you plan on doing the extra-time activity, you'll need elastic cord, pony beads, and fine-tipped permanent markers.

Before class, prepare the secret-flap box you'll need for this object talk. Take an empty cereal box and trace the wide side of the box on a sheet of thin poster board. Cut out the poster-board piece and slide it into the box. Place the flap along the wide side of the box and tape it to the bottom of the box to make a secret flap. (You'll be slyly flipping this flap back and forth one time.) Write the following names for

8

the Holy Spirit on slips of paper, one name per slip: Spirit of truth, Spirit of glory, Counselor, Spirit of God, Holy Spirit, Spirit of wisdom and understanding, Spirit of counsel and power, and Spirit of knowledge. Hold back the slip with "Holy Spirit" written on it, but place the other slips in the secret flap. During the object talk, you'll hold the secret flap slyly closed as you drop the slip of paper with "Holy Spirit" written on it into the main portion of the box. As you talk, you'll shift the flap to the other side of the box, trapping the "Holy Spirit" paper and revealing the other slips of paper, which you'll pour from the box. It will appear as if one name has turned into many! (Hint: Practice this trick several times to make your presentation and flap sliding smooth!)

Discover 'n Do!

Gather kids and hold up the cereal box. (Be sure you've already hidden the names for the Holy Spirit in the secret flap and have the paper with "Holy Spirit" written on it beside you.) Invite kids to tell you different names they have for this type of food. Suggestions might include cereal, breakfast food, breakfast cereal, or specific types such as corn flakes. Say: **There are many names for this type of food. Some of the names describe the food, such as breakfast cereal. Some of the names tell what the food contains, such as corn flakes or rice puffs. And some of the names might even tell what the food does for us, such as Energy-Boosters Granola Bars. Here's another name to read.**

Have a volunteer read the slip of paper with "Holy Spirit" written on it. Quickly show kids the inside of the "empty" box (be sure to hold the secret flap tightly). Say: **This box might seem empty, but when we add the Holy Spirit** (drop in the slip of paper with "Holy Spirit" written on it, then slyly slide the flap over to trap this slip of paper), **amazing things happen! We discover many names for the special friend and teacher Jesus sent us!** Tip the box upside down and allow the remaining slips of paper to tumble out on the floor, then set the box (with the Holy Spirit paper still trapped inside) off to one side.

Say: **Wow! From one name come many! And just as the many names for cereal tell us about the food, the many names for the Holy Spirit teach us about who he is. So what are other names for the Holy Spirit, and what do they teach us about him? Let's see if we can solve the case with a little detective work and the Bible!**

Collect the Clues!

Have kids form seven groups and hand each group a slip of paper containing a name for the Holy Spirit. Explain that you'll take turns reading verses and when a group's name is read, that group can shout, "There's power in the name!" Read the following verses and wait for kids' responses. Then have groups read the names on their slips of paper aloud.

✔ *Matthew 3:16* (Spirit of God)
✔ *John 14:17* (Spirit of truth)
✔ *John 14:26* (Counselor)

✔ **_1 Peter 4:14_** (Spirit of glory)

✔ **_Isaiah 11:2_** (Spirit of wisdom and understanding; Spirit of counsel and power; and Spirit of knowledge)

After the verses and names have been read aloud, ask:

✔ **How do different names for the Holy Spirit help us know him better?**

✔ **Why do you think there are different names for the same Spirit?**

✔ **How can we thank and praise the Holy Spirit in many ways for being our helper, teacher, counselor, and friend?**

Say: **God has many names, which include Father, Lord, Almighty, and Everlasting. Jesus also has different names, which include Savior, Son, Prince of Peace, and Christ the Lord. Just as these names teach us about God's and Jesus' power, so do the different names of the Holy Spirit. But one thing is for sure—although there are many ways to praise the Holy Spirit and many names he is known by, there is only one Spirit who was sent by Jesus to love and guide us and stay right beside us!** Close by saying: **Good for you—you've solved the clues! The Holy Spirit is also called God's Spirit, the Spirit of truth, the Spirit of glory, and Counselor. The case is closed!**

If there's time, let kids make Holy Spirit ID bracelets, ankle bracelets, or necklaces. Have each child choose her favorite name for the Holy Spirit and string as many beads as there are letters in the name on a length of elastic cord. (For longer names, have kids make necklaces.) Use a fine-tipped permanent marker to write the name for the Holy Spirit on the beads, one letter per bead. Then have kids share their projects by reading aloud the names for the Holy Spirit and telling why their chosen names are their favorites.

3-IN-1 SPIRIT POWER!

Judges 14:6; Acts 1:8; Romans 8:14; Galatians 5:22

The Case: *How does the Holy Spirit help us?*

Simple Supplies: You'll need a Bible, a small rubber band, a permanent marker, white paper, tape, and three 10-inch, solid-colored squares of thin cotton or silk. If you plan on doing the extra-time activity, you'll need permanent markers plus a small rubber band and three 8-inch squares of thin fabric for each child.

Before class, prepare and practice this awesome trick to make your presentation smooth. First, you'll need three 10-inch squares of very thin cotton or thin silk fabric. (For a more colorful presentation, choose different colors of fabric!) Using the permanent marker, draw a thick letter "P" in the center of each fabric square. Now that your fabric is ready, here's how to do the trick: Just before the presentation, twist a rubber band fairly tightly around the thumb and forefinger of your right hand.

10

(Keep the fingers with the rubber band hidden, moving, or holding silk squares so no one notices the rubber band.) After showing kids the three separate silk squares, you'll count them as you pass each square into your right hand. As you do this, slyly slip one end of each square into the rubber band. When all three squares are in your hand, roll them like you're making a ball, then have kids count to three and toss the squares in the air, at which point they'll look as if they've been amazingly knotted into one square! After the object talk, kids will enjoy making their own 3-in-1 squares to take home and present to their families and friends. Finally, tape a sheet of paper to the wall or door and have a marker handy.

Discover 'n Do!

Be sure you have the rubber band twisted around the thumb and forefinger of your right hand. Then seat kids a few feet in front of you and say: **We've learned already that the Holy Spirit is part of God's three-in-one team that consists of God the Father, Jesus the Son, and the Holy Spirit. But the Holy Spirit is a three-in-one powerhouse all by himself, too! Let's say that these three squares each represent one quality the Holy Spirit brings to us.** Hold up one square and show kids the letter P. Say: **This letter P stands for the power of the Holy Spirit.** Hold up another square and say: **This P stands for the purpose the Holy Spirit brings to our lives.** Hold up the third square and say: **And this letter P stands for the patience the Holy Spirit brings to us.**

As you continue, begin passing the squares to your hand and sliding their corners under the rubber band. Say: **One portion of the Spirit is power, one portion is purpose, and one portion is patience. That makes three in one and** (toss the squares into the air and let them drop as one unit, but keep the rubber band on the squares still hidden from the kids) **ONE in three! Just as the Holy Spirit, Jesus, and God are three-in-one, so the Holy Spirit is a kind of three-in-one. But how does the Spirit combine three powerful ways to help us, and what exactly are those ways? Let's see if we can solve the case with a little detective work and the Bible!** Set the squares aside for now.

Collect the Clues!

Be sure you've taped a sheet of paper to the wall or door and gather kids in front of the paper. Divide the paper into three columns and label one "Power," another one "Purpose," and the last one "Patience." Then read the following verses and have kids decide whether the verse teaches us about the Spirit's power or how he brings us purpose or patience. The suggested answers are given in parentheses.

✔ *Judges 14:6a; 1 Samuel 10:6; Acts 1:8* (power)
✔ *Romans 5:3-5; Galatians 5:22* (patience)
✔ *Romans 8:14; Philippians 2:1, 2* (purpose)

After you've discussed the verses and where they fit on your chart, write: "We receive POWER from the Holy Spirit" in the first column, "We have a purpose in life through the Holy Spirit" in the second column, and "The Holy Spirit helps us

have patience" in the last column. Ask volunteers to read aloud each sentence, then ask:

- ✔ **How does it strengthen our faith to know we receive power from the Holy Spirit?**
- ✔ **How does the Holy Spirit help us accomplish God's will and purpose for us?**
- ✔ **In what ways does having patience through the Spirit allow us to wait on God's answers better?**

Say: **These three P's of the Holy Spirit—power, purpose, and patience—all help us live our lives the way God desires. We can use the power given to us by remaining strong in our faith. We know we have a purpose and destiny to fulfill in God's plans through the Holy Spirit. And the patience we nurture through the Holy Spirit allows us to wait on God's answers and blessings with perseverance and hope.**

Close by saying: **Good for you—you've solved the clues! The Holy Spirit helps us in three powerful ways, through power, purpose, and patience. This case is closed!**

If there's time, show kids how your opening illusion was done. Then invite kids to make the three squares by writing large letter "P's" on their fabric squares. Hand kids each a rubber band and let them practice attaching the corners of the squares and tossing the three squares to make one. Challenge kids to present this nifty object talk at home as a reminder of the unique three-in-one quality of the Holy Spirit's help.

INE FRUIT

Galatians 5:22, 23; Colossians 3:12-14

The Case: *What kind of fruit does the Spirit help us grow?*

Simple Supplies: You'll need a Bible, construction paper, scissors, tape, paper, markers, fishing line, and newspapers. If you plan on doing the extra-time activity, you'll need napkins, prepared sugar cookies, softened cream cheese, plastic knives, and a variety of chopped fruit such as grapes, apple bits, bananas, pears, and maraschino cherries. (If you desire, you can also use bags of dried fruit bits.)

Before class, cut sixteen 2-inch construction-paper fruit shapes, such as apples, bananas, grapes, oranges, pears, lemons, and limes. Write the following words on the fruit, one word per fruit: compassion, humility, forgiveness, joy, peace, goodness, faithfulness, self-control. On the remaining fruit shapes, write each word on two shapes: love, kindness, gentleness, patience. Tape the fruit shapes along a 3-foot length of fishing line. Tape the first shape several inches from the end of the fishing

line. Now place several sheets of newspaper in a pile and roll them into a cone. Tape the side seam so the cone retains its shape. Between the top layers of newspaper, slide the fishing line and fruit shapes so they're hidden in the sides of the cone. Tape the longer end of the fishing line to the edge of the cone. (Only you will know this bit of fishing line is there!) During the object talk, you'll show kids the "empty" cone. Then at the appropriate time, slyly untape the fishing line and pull the fruit shapes from the empty cone! (This is very impressive!) If there's time after the talk, kids will prepare mini fruit pizzas to nibble as they further discuss the fine fruit the Holy Spirit helps us have in our lives. (Hint: Keep the edges of the cone by the taped fishing line pinched shut as you turn the cone upside down during the object talk.)

Discover 'n Do!

Hold the cone with the fruit shapes hidden in the folds of the cone. Quickly turn the cone around, upside down, and briefly show kids the empty insides. Then say: **What am I holding? Does it look very interesting or usable?** Allow time for kids to respond, then continue: **I'm holding an empty paper cone that doesn't seem so very special. You know, we all feel that way at one time or another. We may feel plain, uninteresting, and as if we have nothing very special to offer God or others. In other words, we may often feel like an empty old paper cone. But wait! Just because you can't see it doesn't mean this cone is so plain and unusable. It's really holding a treasure inside!** Quickly untape the fishing line and pull out the line of paper fruit shapes as if you're pulling them from the inside of the cone.

Say: **Whoa! There was a lot more to this old paper cone than we thought! That's how it is when we trust and love the Holy Spirit. The Spirit brings more to our lives and hearts than first meets the eye. We may not feel changed on the outside, but, oh, what the Spirit gives us on the inside! Let's see what fine fruit the Holy Spirit helps place in our lives.**

Invite kids to read aloud the words on the pieces of paper fruit, then say: **These are wonderful fruits the Holy Spirit helps us grow in our lives. But what does this fine fruit do for us, and why does the Spirit help us grow these things in our hearts and lives? Let's see if we can be "fruitful" and solve this case with a little detective work and the Bible!**

Collect the Clues!

Have kids form small groups of three or four and hand each group a sheet of paper and marker. Challenge groups to read the following verses and list the fine fruit the Spirit wants us to have in our lives: Galatians 5:22, 23 and Colossians 3:12-14. (The fruit from these two references should match the sixteen fruit shapes you pulled from the paper cone.) After the lists have been made, have kids come together to compare their discoveries and briefly discuss why each fruit is important to loving God and serving others. Then ask:

✔ **Which fine fruits are mentioned in both references? Why do you think they were named two times?**

✔ **Can we truly love and obey God without these fruits in our hearts and lives? Explain.**

✔ **Why do you think the Holy Spirit wants to help us grow these qualities and attitudes in our hearts and lives?**

✔ **How can we grow these good qualities in our lives?**

Say: **Before we came to know the Holy Spirit and welcome him into our lives, we were like that empty paper cone—not full and pretty useless to be used by God. But once we have the Holy Spirit to guide us, our lives and hearts become filled with fine fruit we can use to serve God and others and can pass along to others. What happens when you plant more fruit seeds from good fruit? It grows into even more fine fruit! And that's just what the Holy Spirit wants for us! When we put our fine fruit to work in our relation-ships with God and others, the fruit multiplies and becomes even sweeter.** Close by saying: **Good for you—you've solved the clues! The Holy Spirit helps us grow good qualities and attitudes that help us serve God and others more fruitfully. This case is closed!**

If there's time, let kids prepare yummy mini fruit pizzas by spreading softened cream cheese on sugar cookies, then topping the cookie pizzas with fruit bits. As kids nibble their treats, have them discuss more ways to grow and use these fine fruits to serve God and others.

PATIENCE TO BLOW

Psalms 27:14; 33:20; 37:34; Romans 8:25, 26; 15:5

The Case: *How does the Holy Spirit help us persevere?*

Simple Supplies: You'll need a Bible, a thumb tack, index cards, markers, and a large, empty spool of thread (the kind with one hole). If you plan on doing the extra-time craft activity, you'll also need an empty spool of thread, index card, and thumbtack for each child.

Before class, prepare and practice this cool demonstration of patience and per-severance. First, hold the index card to the bottom of the spool and blow steadily through the hole in the spool. Let go of the card and it will flutter to the floor. Now stick the thumbtack through the center of the index card. Lean forward and blow steadily as you place the point of the thumbtack through the hole in the spool. Hold the card firmly in this position for a few seconds and continue to blow. If you're

14

blowing firmly and steadily, the card will stay in place on the spool after you let go! (Neat, isn't it?) Use a new index card when you're ready to begin the object talk in class. Kids will be decorating their own spools and index cards to accompany this object talk for the extra-time activity. Be sure to have colorful markers ready. If the spools are plastic, use permanent markers. (Hint: The trick to making the card stick is to blow through the spool with long, steady breaths.)

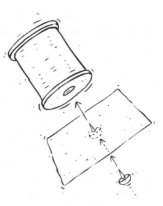

Discover 'n Do!

Place the thumbtack on a table and hold the index card and spool. Explain to kids that you want to try a new trick you've learned but that you are having a bit of trouble getting it to work. Keep trying to make the index card stick to the spool while blowing through the hole and letting the card fall to the floor. After several attempts, say: **Whew! It's not easy to have patience and perseverance when you're learning something new, is it? What other things take patience and "stick-to-itiveness"?** Allow time for kids to respond. Suggestions might include learning a new language, waiting for answers to prayer, and even keeping strong faith! Then say: **It's not always easy to have patience and perseverance, especially when it comes to keeping strong faith and steady hope. For example, we may run out of patience waiting for God to answer our prayers, or maybe our perseverance runs short as we try to learn God's Word or get through troubles and worries. Let's face it—we need a big boost when it comes to patience and perseverance! But who can help give us the boost of stick-to-itiveness we need? The Holy Spirit can!**

Hold up the thumbtack and say: **When we have the Holy Spirit in the center of our lives** (push the thumbtack through the center of the index card), **he helps us have patience and perseverance to stick to anything!** Use the thumbtack to accomplish your feat of stick-to-itiveness, then say: **Wow! The Holy Spirit gives us that boost of perseverance and patience we need! But how does the Spirit help us persevere, and why does he want us to be patient? Let's see if we can solve this case with a little detective work and the Bible!**

Collect the Clues!

Say: **We are discovering that the Holy Spirit can do many things for us, and one of the most powerful ways he helps us is through giving us perseverance and patience. Let's explore why the Spirit of God wants us to have perseverance.** Invite volunteers to read aloud the following verses: Psalms 27:14; 33:20; 37:34; and Proverbs 20:22. Then ask:

✔ **Why do you think it is important to wait on the Lord's answers and help?**

✔ **What might happen if we give up before God chooses to answer us?**

✔ **What can we do while we wait on God?**

Say: **As we wait on God, for his answers or help, we can keep obeying him, praising him, and praying—and the Holy Spirit helps us do these things! Let's see how else the Holy Spirit helps us have patience.** Read aloud Romans 8:25 and 26a. Ask:

✔ **How are patience and hope connected to one another?**

✔ **In what ways does the Spirit help us hold on to hope when we are weak and want to give up?**

Say: **The Holy Spirit helps us hold on to hope by keeping us praying and thanking God for his answers even before he chooses to answer our prayers! Remember: The Holy Spirit is also the Spirit of God and knows what we need and want even before we do. And the Spirit helps us pray to God and wait for his answers. In these ways, the Holy Spirit gives our perseverance and patience a real boost!**

Push the thumbtack through the index card again and make the card stick to the spool as you blow for several seconds. Then say: **When we keep the Holy Spirit in the center of our lives, he will give us the stick-to-itiveness we need to have powerful patience and perseverance.** Close by saying: **Good for you—you've solved the clues! The Spirit helps us have patience and perseverance to wait on God. The case is closed!** Read aloud Romans 15:5 to end your object-talk time.

For an extra-time activity, let kids decorate their own spools and index cards so they can present this awesome object talk at home for their families and friends. Use colorful markers to decorate large empty spools. Then have kids write *"Wait for the LORD; be strong and take heart and wait for the LORD" (Psalm 27:14)* on their index cards, then decorate and embellish the cards. Hand out thumbtacks and show kids how to make the cards stick to the spools. Remind kids that the Holy Spirit gives us patience and perseverance to learn new tricks as well as wait on the Lord!

S PREAD OUT!

Luke 12:12; John 16:13; 2 Peter 1:21

The Case: *Why does the Holy Spirit help us tell others about Jesus?*

Simple Supplies: You'll need a Bible, three clear bowls of water, pepper, and liquid dishwashing soap. If you plan on doing the extra-time craft activity, you'll need white self-adhesive paper, colorful permanent markers, and a paper salt-and-pepper shaker for each child. (These shakers are available in the picnic aisles at grocery stores. They're disposable salt-and-pepper shakers to set on picnic tables.)

Before class, try this simple trick at home to become familiar with how it works. Fill a clear bowl with water and sprinkle pepper in the center of the water where

it will stay in a floating "clump." Now place a dab of dishwashing liquid on your fingertip. When you place your fingertip in the center of the pepper, the black dots will race for the edges of the bowl! You'll demonstrate this "spicy race" a few times, so have three clear bowls of water ready. (Have the dishwashing liquid on your finger before the object talk to make it look as if you are "controlling" the pepper through your own power.) For the extra-time activity, kids will be making neat salt-and-pepper shakers to use at home as reminders of telling others about Jesus through the help of the Holy Spirit.

Discover 'n Do!

Place the three clear bowls of water on a table and have the pepper close by. (Be sure you have a dab of liquid dishwashing soap secretly on your finger!) Gather kids around the bowls and say: **Let's pretend this bowl is the world and this pepper is wonderful news we want to spread.** (Shake pepper in the center of the first two bowls.) **This is the wonderful truth about Jesus that God's Word tells us to spread. It's the truth about Jesus being God's only heavenly Son and about how he died and was raised to life again to forgive our sins. We want to spread the Good News, but how?** (Stick a finger without the soap into the center of the pepper in one bowl, then hold up your finger.) **Sometimes we try to spread the Good News, but it doesn't work or others won't listen, and instead of spreading the Word, it just gets stuck. But when we trust the Holy Spirit to touch our hearts and words** (touch the fingertip with the soap to the center of the pepper in the second bowl), **God's Word and truth spread like lightning! But what is it about the Holy Spirit that helps us tell others the Good News about Jesus, and how does the Spirit help us spread God's truth to others? Let's see if we can solve the case with a little detective work and the Bible!** (You'll use the third bowl a bit later in the object talk.)

Collect the Clues!

Invite kids to read aloud the following verses, then ask the questions below: Luke 12:12; John 16:13; and 2 Peter 1:21.

- ✔ **Why do you think the Holy Spirit will give you the words to say when telling someone about Jesus?**
- ✔ **How can telling others the truth about Jesus help them? draw us closer to the Lord?**
- ✔ **In what ways does knowing that the Holy Spirit guides us in all truth help us have faith in God's Word?**

Say: **There are so many wonderful things to tell others about Jesus! What are things you could tell?** Allow kids time to share what they

17

would tell others about Jesus. Suggestions might include that Jesus is God's only Son, that Jesus is fully God and fully human, that Jesus came to love us and forgive our sins, that Jesus offers us eternal life if we accept him into our lives, and that Jesus teaches us how to love and obey God.

Say: **The Holy Spirit knows what others need to learn about Jesus. And the Holy Spirit also knows that sometimes we find the words hard to say or explain. That's why God's Spirit promises to give us the right words to say at the best time. It makes me feel great to know I can rely on the Holy Spirit to help me tell others about Jesus! And just imagine what would happen if all of us gathered in class today** (sprinkle pepper in the center of the third clear bowl of water and slyly put another dab of soap on your fingertip and touch the center of the pepper) **ran to tell others about Jesus. Just think of all the power and truth that would go out into the world! When we trust the Holy Spirit to help us tell others about Jesus, the word really gets around!** Close by saying: **Good for you—you've solved the clues! The Holy Spirit helps us spread the Good News about Jesus by giving us the right words to say at just the right time. This case is closed!**

If there's time, kids will enjoy making special salt-and-pepper shakers to use at home during their family meals. Let kids cut white self-adhesive paper labels to fit around the shakers. Before peeling off the paper backing and sticking the labels in place, have kids write *"For the Holy Spirit will teach you at that time what you should say" (Luke 12:12)* on one shaker label, and *"But when he, the Spirit of truth, comes, he will guide you into all truth" (John 16:13)* on the other label. Decorate the labels, then stick them in place by peeling off the paper backing. Encourage kids to use these shakers during family meals as they discuss what the Spirit urges us to tell others about Jesus.

PROBLEM SOLVED

Numbers 11:17; John 3:34; 2 Timothy 1:14

The Case: *Why does the Holy Spirit help with our problems?*

Simple Supplies: You'll need a Bible, a shaker of salt, paper plates, and an ice cube and 10-inch length of yarn or string for each person. If you plan on doing the extra-time activity, you'll also need several skeins of yarn, craft glue, water, plastic bowls, waxed paper, small balloons, glitter, and scissors.

Before class, try this cool trick to become familiar with how it works. (You'll need an ice cube for yourself and one for each child during the object talk.) Place an ice cube on a paper plate and hold a length of yarn or string as you contemplate how to lift the ice using the yarn and without tying the yarn in a knot. Seems impossible, doesn't it? Well, here's the trick: Simply coil one end of the string or yarn on top of

the ice cube, then pour about a quarter teaspoon of salt over the coiled end of the
yarn and count slowly to fifteen. When you gently lift the yarn, it will be stuck to the
ice—voilà, the ice cube is suspended! Kids will be doing this object talk alongside
you. After the object-talk time, kids will enjoy making glittery yarn ornaments using
the yarn from this object talk. (Hint: Pour on enough salt and wait for fifteen to
twenty seconds before gently lifting the ice cube.)

Discover 'n Do!

Distribute the paper plates, ice cubes, and pieces of yarn or string. (Be sure you have an ice cube, string or yarn, and paper plate for yourself as well. Set the salt off to one side.) Explain that you want to solve the problem of how to lift an ice cube without touching the ice or tying a knot in the yarn. Ask kids to tell their ideas and try them with their own ice cubes. After a few moments, say: **There are different things here to help solve this problem. There are plates, ice cubes, yarns, and lots of people to brainstorm and offer their thoughts and opinions. But without a secret ingredient, this problem is nearly impossible to solve! Watch and see how a simple yet powerful ingredient solves this icy problem!**

Curl the yarn on top of the ice cube, then add the salt. Have kids count to fifteen or twenty with you, then lift the yarn and cube. Say: **Wow! Our problem has been solved in an amazing way with our secret ingredient: salt! We have many problems in our lives that need to be solved, too. There may be things that seem to help or people who offer their assistance or best wishes, but without our special spiritual "secret ingredient," many problems can't be solved. Who's our spiritual secret ingredient? The Holy Spirit, of course! Through the power of the Holy Spirit, our problems are lighter and worries become brighter. But why does the Spirit want our problems to be solved, and what can he do to help? Let's see if we can solve the case with a little detective work and the Bible!**

Let kids coil their yarns and add salt to their ice cubes to lift them before moving on to the Bible exploration.

Collect the Clues!

Say: **God sent his Spirit through Jesus to be our helper and friend, our counselor and guide. And there's no one better than the Holy Spirit at helping us solve the problems we encounter. Let's see how God sent the Spirit to help his people and Moses long ago.** Read aloud Numbers 11:17, then ask:

    ✔ **Why do you think God knew we needed help with our burdens and troubles?**

    ✔ **How does relying on the Holy Spirit's help get us through problems? help strengthen our faith?**

Say: **God's Word assures us that we have help through the Holy Spirit. Let's read three verses and put them into our own words to explain what the Spirit does for us.** Read aloud the following verses and let kids paraphrase what they've read. (Suggestions are in italics.)

✔ ***Romans 8:26a*** *(The Holy Spirit helps us when we're weak.)*

✔ ***2 Timothy 1:14*** *(Our hope in times of trouble is guarded through the Holy Spirit.)*

✔ ***John 3:34b*** *(God gives us the Holy Spirit as much as we need him; there's no limit to how much help the Spirit can give us.)*

Say: **God has promised us help for problems and troubles through the guidance and assistance of the Holy Spirit. The Spirit is given to us without limit to help in times of trouble. The Holy Spirit brings solutions and clears our hearts and minds so we can see how God is working. And the Holy Spirit freely offers us his help because he knows that problems and worries can keep us from serving God. Isn't it great to have a spiritual secret ingredient to help us solve our problems?**

Close by saying: **Good for you—you've solved the clues! The Holy Spirit helps us solve the worries and problems that keep us from loving and serving God. Yea, Spirit! This case is closed!**

If there's time, let kids make glittery ornaments using the yarn or string from the object talk (plus extra yarn you provide). For each ornament, blow up and knot a small balloon. Cut 10-inch lengths of yarn or string and dip them in bowls of craft glue that have been thinned with water (about one part water to three parts glue). Wrap the yarn or string around the balloon in every direction, adding more sting or yarn as needed to nearly cover the balloon. Remind kids that just as the yarn covers the balloons, the Holy Spirit covers us with his help and guidance. Sprinkle the sticky yarn with glitter, then place the covered balloons on waxed paper to dry for several hours. (To speed up drying time, use blow dryers.) When the ornaments are completely dry, pop the balloons and remove them. Tie a length of yarn or string to the tops of the ornaments so they can be suspended from windows or doorways.

SPIRIT OF LIFE

John 3:6; 6:63; Romans 8:6, 9, 11, 28; 2 Thessalonians 2:13

The Case: *How does the Holy Spirit bring us life?*

Simple Supplies: You'll need a Bible, paper, markers, tape, and a battery along with three items that use the battery, such as a flashlight, a mechanical toy, and a radio or hand-held electronic game or calculator. (Be sure the same battery works in all three of the items.) If you plan on doing the extra-time activity,

you'll also need a small, inexpensive flashlight and battery for each child plus tacky craft glue and embellishments such as sequins, plastic jewels, and colored aquarium gravel.

Before class, collect the battery and items that use the battery. Remove any other batteries from the items so that during class kids can see that the items are not working (for lack of a battery), then see what happens when the items are "powered up" using the battery. The battery will be likened to how the Holy Spirit gives us life and allows us to do the things we were created to do or meant to accomplish. The battery working in the items will also serve as a way for kids to understand that the Holy Spirit powers up and gives life to each of us in different ways. Have paper and markers handy, since kids will be listing observations about the battery and items in small groups. After the object talk, kids will enjoy decorating and embellishing their own mini flashlights and batteries.

Discover 'n Do!

Have kids form pairs or trios and hand each group of partners a sheet of paper and a marker. Place the three items without their batteries on a table and have kids jot down a few observations about each item. For example, kids might write what the purpose of each item is and what features they observe, such as off-on switches or light bulbs. After a few minutes, have groups compare their observations. Then say: **You're all fine detectives! I know now what each item is supposed to do, so let's see if they work!** Turn each item on, and when it doesn't hop to life, make comments such as, "What could be wrong here?" and "Why does this item seem dead and lifeless?" Lead kids to suggest checking the battery, then ask volunteers to try the battery in each item to see if it can power up the items.

When all the items have hopped to life using the battery, remove the battery and hold it up. Say: **Wow! This battery brings life and purpose to each of these items. Without it, the items are useless and will never be used according to their purpose. This is just what the Holy Spirit does for us. When we have the Holy Spirit in our lives, he powers us to be used by God in amazing ways—ways that God has already planned for us. And just as this battery worked to make each item do different things, the Holy Spirit works in each of us differently, too. But how does the Spirit bring us life, and what can we accomplish when the Holy Spirit lives in us? Let's see if we can solve the case with a little more detective work and the Bible!**

Collect the Clues!

Tape a sheet of paper to the wall or door and ask a volunteer to draw a large, simple outline of a battery on the paper. Write the words "Powered by" above the drawing and the words "the Holy Spirit" below the drawing. Then read aloud the following verses about the way the Holy Spirit brings us life and about God's purpose for us. List your discoveries on the battery drawing. Read aloud John 3:6, 34; 6:63; Romans 8:6, 9, 11, 28; and 2 Thessalonians 2:13. After listing your discoveries, ask:

✔ In what ways does the Holy Spirit give us life? help us accomplish God's purposes for us?

✔ How is a spiritual life different from a physical life? Which life lasts forever? Explain.

✔ In what ways does the Holy Spirit power up our spiritual lives?

✔ Why is it good that the Holy Spirit works in each of us differently?

✔ How can we be more open to allowing the Spirit of God to work in us?

Say: **We've made some very important discoveries today! We've discovered that the Holy Spirit brings us life and powers us to do God's will. We've explored what being powered up by the Spirit does for us. And we've learned that, just as items without batteries don't "come to life" and are not useable, without the Holy Spirit in our lives we are not able to be used fully by God! Our parents gave us physical life, but the Spirit of God gives us spiritual life and powers us up to be used by God.**

Close by saying: **Good for you—you've solved the clues! The Holy Spirit is like our ever-ready, always-steady battery that gives us life and powers us to be used by God. This case is closed!**

If there's time, let kids embellish their own mini flashlights. Use tacky craft glue to glue sequins, plastic jewels, and colored aquarium gravel to small plastic flashlights. As kids work, remind them that, just like flashlights need batteries to power them up and give them life, we're not useable until we have the life and power of the Holy Spirit in us. Hand kids batteries to power up their flashlights.

PRAY TODAY!

Romans 8:26, 27; Ephesians 6:18; Jude 20

The Case: *How is prayer affected by the Holy Spirit?*

Simple Supplies: You'll need a Bible, newspapers, and six 2-inch hearts cut from red construction paper. If you plan on doing the extra-time activity, you'll need index cards, colorful markers, scissors, glue, and copies of the poem from this activity (page 24).

Before class, cut out six red construction-paper hearts. Make the hearts about 2 inches wide so kids can easily see them. Lay several sheets of newspaper on top of each other, then roll the pile of papers into an elongated cone shape. Tape the cone along the sides so it stays together. Notice how there are several layers of paper at the top of the cone? These layers form hidden "pockets" into which you'll slyly slide three of the paper hearts during the object talk. The other hearts will be hidden before class someplace in the room. During the object talk, you'll visit about how our prayers are like gifts we box and wrap to present to God, at which point you'll slide three paper hearts into the folds at the top of the cone. (Kids will think you're plac-

ing the hearts into the body of the cone.) Then, when you
turn the cone upside down to "deliver" the prayers to God,
the cone will be empty! (Tightly pinch the upper edges of
the cone together to keep the hearts from fluttering free!)
At the appointed time, retrieve the hidden paper hearts, and
it will appear as if the hearts escaped or got through the sides of
the cone—just as the Holy Spirit helps our prayers get through to
God. If there's time after the object talk, kids will enjoy making
Prayer Postcards to remind them that the Holy Spirit intercedes
for us in prayer.

Discover 'n Do!

Before kids come to class, hide three of the paper hearts in a
place where kids won't find them. Hold up the other three paper
hearts and the paper cone. Say: **Let's pretend these paper hearts
are the prayers we offer to God each time we talk to him. When
we offer prayers to God, it's like giving God special gifts. We wrap
our prayers with love and place them in our hearts.** As you continue, slyly
place the paper hearts in the upper folds of the cone, but make it appear as if you're
really placing the hearts in the cone itself. Continue: **But have you ever prayed
and then waited for God to answer and thought that perhaps God never
received your prayers? Or have you worried that you didn't pray right or
use the best words so that your prayers just vanished into thin air?** Turn the
cone upside down and shake it so kids see that the prayers have "vanished." Say:
**Wow! Where do our prayers go? Do they really make it to God, and if so,
how do they reach him even when we can't find the words to pray? Let's
see if we can solve the case of the disappearing prayers with a little detective work and the Bible!**

Collect the Clues!

Form three small groups and assign each group one of the following passages to
look up, read, and discuss: Romans 8:26, 27; Ephesians 6:18; and Jude 20. Have kids
briefly discuss what the verses teach about who helps us pray and how we should
pray. Then come back as a whole group and share the verses aloud as well as the
discoveries. Then ask:

✔ **Who helps us when we're too weak, sad, or troubled to find the words
to pray?**

✔ **Why do you think the Holy Spirit helps us pray and come closer to God?**

✔ **How is the Holy Spirit's help in praying a demonstration of his love
for us?**

Say: **We have a special interpreter in the Holy Spirit. Just as if you had a
friend who couldn't ask for help but you asked for him, the Holy Spirit goes
to God on our behalf. This is called "intercession," and we know that the
Holy Spirit intercedes for us when we pray. That means the Spirit carries**

our prayers to God and even tells God what we mean to say and want to pray! Hold the "empty" cone upside down again and say: **When we pray with the help of the Holy Spirit, we can be assured that our prayers never vanish into thin air.** (Set down the cone and walk across the room to retrieve the three paper hearts.) **They reach the heart and ears of God every time!**

Close by saying: **Good for you—you've solved the clues! The Holy Spirit interprets and intercedes for us whenever we pray so we can trust each prayer we say reaches God with love and praise! This case is closed!**

If there's time, let kids make several Prayer Postcards to use during those times when prayers may be hard to express. Make several copies of the poem box from this activity for each child. Then let kids cut out the poems and glue them to index cards to make postcards. Decorate the sides of the cards with poems. As kids work, explain that these cards can be used whenever it seems difficult to talk to God in regular prayers. Kids can use the other sides of the cards to write special messages to God, to compose poems to him, or to draw pictures of how they feel. Encourage kids to look up and read the verses below the poem each time they use their Prayer Postcards.

Please, Holy Spirit, help me pray
And express to God what I cannot say.
Carry my prayers on wings like a dove
And take them to God with all of my love.
(Romans 8:26, 27; Jude 20)

Please, Holy Spirit, help me pray
And express to God what I cannot say.
Carry my prayers on wings like a dove
And take them to God with all of my love.
(Romans 8:26, 27; Jude 20)

SPIRIT SIGHT

1 Timothy 4:1; 1 John 4:1, 2, 6; Jude 18-20

The Case: *What is discernment?*

Simple Supplies: You'll need a Bible, markers, and a cardboard tube (such as bathroom tissue tubes or sectioned paper-towel tubes) for each person plus one extra. In this activity, the extra-time craft and object talk are all rolled into one, so you won't need extra items.

Before class, make sure you have a cardboard tube for each person plus one extra for you. You can use empty bathroom tissue tubes or cut paper-towel tubes in half. Cardboard tubes from wrapping paper work well, and you can get about four tubes from each one! If all else fails, make tubes using poster board and tape the sides securely. Practice this simple—yet simply awesome—object talk so you get the hang of how to "look through" your hand as if you have X-ray vision. To do this, hold the tube in your left hand and place your right hand, palm facing you, beside the tube. Stare straight ahead between the tube and your hand. If you're in the correct position, an optical illusion will make it seem as if you're seeing right through your hand! (Very neat, isn't it? And kids will love this trick!) Kids will be coloring their tubes and peeking through them to learn about what it means to have discernment through the Holy Spirit. Have lots of brightly colored markers ready!

Discover 'n Do!

Have kids form small groups and be sure each group has plenty of colorful markers. Distribute the tubes and say: **We're going to make some awesome X-ray vision tubes to help us see through our hands and even see through our friends! You can color and decorate your tube as we chat a bit about seeing through other people to tell whether they're honest or phonies we want to avoid.** As kids color their tubes, ask:

✔ **How can you tell if someone is being honest or not?**
✔ **Why is it good to be careful about the people we hang out with or choose to be friends with?**
✔ **Are all people we meet kind, honest-type people? Explain.**

Have kids put down their markers and assure them they can finish decorating later if needed. Say: **Now let's have a bit of fun seeing if we have X-ray vision and can see through things with our special tubes.** Show kids how to see through their hands using their X-ray tubes. Then see if they can see through a friend's hand or even his head!

After playing with the tubes for several minutes, have kids set their X-ray tubes down. Say: **That was fun, wasn't it? There is a saying about being able to "see through" someone when that person is not being honest or good-hearted. What do you think it means to "see through" someone?** Allow kids time to share their ideas, then say: **Being able to see through someone doesn't mean we can actually see through someone's body; it means that we have a strong feeling if that person is being sincere, honest, and the kind of person we want to be associated with. Some people claim to like other people, but they don't act that way, and we can see through them. Others claim to be telling the truth, but often we can see through their lies and know the real truth. And other people claim they love the Lord, but their actions say otherwise. Being able to "see through" someone is called "discernment." Discernment means being on our guard to tell if someone is truthful and truly loves God. God wants us to have discernment, but how do we get it? Can the Holy Spirit help us discern truth from lies and honest people from phonies? Let's see if we can solve the case with a little detective work and the Bible!**

Collect the Clues!

Say: **Let's begin by discovering what the Bible says about testing spirits to see if they're really from God. We'll also see how the Holy Spirit helps us discern good from bad.** Read aloud 1 Timothy 4:1; 1 John 4:1, 2, 6; and Jude 18-20. Then ask:

✔ **Is there a need for discerning if someone or something is from God? Explain.**

✔ **How does God's Spirit help us tell good from evil and truth from lies?**

✔ **Why is it important to trust the Holy Spirit to help us discern good from evil?**

✔ **What might happen if we didn't use discernment and if we trusted everyone and everything people said?**

Say: **God warned us that there would be people who are not of him and that they would try to mislead us. It's very important, then, to trust the Holy Spirit in helping us discern good from evil and to help us see through lies to get to the truth. We talk about "seeing through" people and lies, and so does the Bible. What do you think this verse is saying?** Read aloud Proverbs 28:11, then have kids tell what they think the verse is saying about seeing through to the truth in people.

Say: **God wants us to test the spirits and to make sure they are from him. God wants us to use discernment when dealing with people and to see through lies so we always have the truth. Isn't it awesome that the Holy Spirit gives us spiritual X-ray vision? Let's write 1 John 4:1 on our X-ray vision tubes to remind us that the Holy Spirit helps us see through to the truth!**

Have kids write the first portion of 1 John 4:1 on their tubes, then close by saying: **Good for you—you've solved the clues! Discernment is seeing through to the truth and understanding that not everything is good or from God. And the Holy Spirit helps us have the discernment we need each day! This case is closed.**

TERRIFIC TEMPLES

1 Corinthians 3:16, 17; 6:19, 20; Ephesians 2:21, 22

The Case: *How does the Holy Spirit strengthen us to live for God?*

Simple Supplies: You'll need a Bible, two shoe boxes with lids, a brick, duct tape, construction paper, tape, books, and markers. If you plan on doing the extra-time activity, you'll also need self-hardening clay, waxed paper, and craft sticks or pencils to carve the clay.

Before class, collect two shoe boxes with lids. Use duct tape to tape a brick or large stone inside and at one end of one of the shoe boxes. Be sure the brick won't move around inside the box once the lid is taped on. Then tape the lids on both boxes and cover the boxes with the same color of construction paper. Make both boxes look like identical houses by using markers to draw windows, doors, and roofs. Now set the unweighted house on a book with half of the house hanging over the edge. Of course the house will topple over when you let go. But when you place the weighted end of the other house on the book, the house should not topple over but stay secure with its end hanging off of the book and seeming to defy gravity. You'll use these houses to help kids understand what it means to be temples of the Lord and how the Holy Spirit helps us become those temples as we live for God. If there's time after the object talk, kids will love making their own special cornerstones as reminders to live their lives as temples unto God. Be sure you have plenty of self-hardening clay for kids to form their cornerstones.

Discover 'n Do!

Place two books on a table and set the two houses beside the books so kids can see them without lifting them up. (Keep in mind which house has the weight inside

and which end is weighted!) Ask kids to look at the two buildings and see if they can tell any difference between the two. Then say: **These buildings look very much alike. We can tell they are both the same size, and both are the same colors, with the same number of windows and doors. But one of these buildings is different and very special! Let me set the buildings on books so you can get a better look.**

Set the box without the weight on one of the books hanging half off, but don't let go yet. Place the weighted end of the other box on the second book, then as you let go of both boxes, say: **Which building is the special one? It's the building that's standing even when it should be falling over! That's because this building has something special inside** (pat the weighted end of the box), **something that gives it substance and makes it stand firm.** Ask:

✔ **In what ways are people like buildings?**

✔ **What must be inside of us to make us strong and give us substance?**

Say: **People all look pretty much alike, just as these buildings do. But some people have something very special inside that makes them stand firm like our building here, even when it seems that troubles would make them tumble apart. That special something inside of these people is the Holy Spirit, and through him we become more than mere "buildings"—we become temples of the Lord! So how does the Holy Spirit strengthen us to live for God, and what does it mean to be a temple of the Lord? Let's see if we can solve this case with a little detective work and the Bible!**

Collect the Clues!

Have kids form small groups and read these verses: 1 Corinthians 3:16, 17; 6:19, 20; and Ephesians 2:21, 22. Then have kids discuss in their groups the answers to the following questions:

✔ **Who lives in us and helps us become a temple unto God?**

✔ **Why does the Spirit protect us when we are God's temple?**

✔ **In what ways are we like a living dwelling for God and his Spirit?**

Say: **As temples of the Lord, we're not built with stones or bricks but by the Holy Spirit who lives in us.** Ask:

✔ **How does knowing we're built with the Spirit in our hearts change the way we live and speak?**

✔ **How are we made stronger by living for God? by having the Holy Spirit live in us?**

Say: **Churches are often thought of as temples, but God's Word tells us that we are his temples, too. When the Holy Spirit lives in us, we are changed to become God's living dwellings, and we live for God in all we say and do. In this way, we can stand firm and strong when other people crumble and fall during tough times. Just like our amazing building that seems to defy gravity, we are God's amazing temples through the Holy Spirit!** Close by saying: **Good for you—you've solved the clues! The Holy Spirit lives in us to strengthen us as living temples to the Lord. The case is closed!**

If there's time, kids will enjoy making special Temple Stones to remind them that they themselves are temples to the Lord. For each stone, have kids mold a tennis-ball lump of self-hardening clay into a 1-inch-thick oval "stone." Use craft sticks, pencils, or toothpicks to write *"Don't you know that you yourselves are God's temple?" (1 Corinthians 3:16a)* on the stones. Let the clay harden for a few days, then have kids use their stones as paperweights, desk decorations, or garden stones.

STOPPED BY THE SPIRIT!

Zechariah 4:6; Acts 1:8; Ephesians 6:17, 18

The Case: *How does the Holy Spirit help us fight evil?*

Simple Supplies: You'll need a Bible, a large sheet of paper, a marker, tape, and a deck of playing cards (number cards only). If you plan on doing the extra-time activity, you'll need colorful markers, tacky craft glue, aluminum foil, glitter, and a sheet of yellow or white poster board for each child.

Before class, prepare and practice this very simple but effective trick. Separate the red and black cards from a deck of playing cards, number cards only. (If you prefer to use another type of playing-card deck, you'll need two colors, such as red and blue or red and yellow cards.) The red cards will represent the fire of the Holy Spirit, and the black (or other color cards) will represent evil or temptations we want to steer clear of. Now here's the important part: Take the pile of red cards in your hands and bend them forward. Then take the black cards and bend them backward. Now shuffle the cards. As you flip through the cards, face down, you'll be able to tell the red from the black by the way they curve. The object of this trick is to pick the red from the black cards without seeing them face up. Kids will be amazed at your unusual skill in choosing the right cards! Before class, tape a sheet of paper to the wall and have a marker handy. If there's time after the object talk, kids will be making Power Posters to remind them of the Spirit's power to stop evil. (Hint: Don't bend the cards so much that your audience notices and be sure to practice enough to know which bend direction indicates both the red and black cards!)

Discover 'n Do!

Be sure you've taped a sheet of paper to the wall or door and have a marker nearby. Gather kids in front of you and hold the red and black cards. Say: **I have a pile of red and black cards here.** (Show kids a red card and a black card.) **Let's say the red cards represent the fire and goodness of the Holy Spirit, and the black cards represent evil acts and bad temptations. We know that both good and bad are mixed up in our world** (shuffle the cards), **and we see both**

every day. God wants us to stay away from evil and temptations. Let's go through this pile of red and black cards and see if we can steer clear of the evil and only save the red ones that represent the fire of the Holy Spirit. I'll tell you, without looking at the card, if it's good or bad. If the card is a good red one, I'll place it to my right and you can hold your thumbs up and give a cheer. But if I correctly identify a card as black, we'll turn it face down and you can give a thumbs-down sign and a big "boo!"

Proceed to turn over the cards and say if a card is red or black according to the curve. Then show the card to the kids and wait for their responses. (Kids will be surprised after you continue to tell the difference between the red cards and the black ones without looking!) When you finish, say: **Wow! And I didn't even have to look at the cards to tell good from bad! Of course, I used a little trick to do this. But in real life, the Holy Spirit does help us stay away from evil and send it away from us in amazing ways. How does the Holy Spirit help us resist temptations and fight evil? Let's see if we can solve this case with a little detective work and the Bible!** Set the cards aside.

Collect the Clues!

Gather kids in front of the paper taped to the wall. Use the marker to divide the paper into three columns and write the word "Who" at the top of one column, the word "What" on the second, and the word "How" on the third. Explain that you'll read aloud verses to discover the answers to who helps us stop evil, what he gives us, and how we can fight evil and resist temptations. Read the following verses and write the answers in the columns under the titles.

✔ *Zechariah 4:6* (who: the Holy Spirit)
✔ *Acts 1:8* (what: power from the Holy Spirit)
✔ *Ephesians 6:17, 18* (how: through remembering our salvation; through God's Word; through praying in the Spirit)

After the columns have been filled in, say: **God knew there would be evil and bad temptations in the world. But God is bigger and more powerful than any evil, and so is his love for us! Because God loves us so greatly, he has provided a way for us to fight evil and resist temptations. The Holy Spirit helps us accomplish this in many ways. The Spirit helps us learn and use God's Word, which is the sword of the Spirit. He helps us resist temptation by giving us discernment so we can tell when something is good and when something is bad—just as we knew with our cards. And the Holy Spirit helps us keep praying and praising God—and where there is God, there can be no darkness or evil!** Ask:

✔ How did God giving us the Holy Spirit to help fight evil show us his love?
✔ Why is it important to rely on the help of the Holy Spirit to fight evil and resist temptations?
✔ Do you think the Holy Spirit will ever let us down when we ask him to help us fight evil? Explain.

Say: **Wow! The Holy Spirit really helps us stop evil and stomp temptations! I'm glad I have the power of the Spirit on my side, aren't you?** Close

by saying: **Good for you—you've solved the clues! The Holy Spirit helps us fight evil through prayer, discernment, his power, and by helping us learn and use God's Word. This case is closed!**

If there's time, let kids make huge Power Posters to remind them that it is through God's Spirit that we can overcome evil and resist temptations. Have kids write Zechariah 4:6 ("'Not by might nor by power, but by my Spirit,' says the LORD Almighty") in large, thick letters on their posters. Then use glitter to outline the letters and add bits of shiny foil to embellish the edges of the posters. Challenge kids to hang the posters in their rooms and to memorize the verse to use in fighting evil and resisting temptations.

READY, WILLING, AND ABLE!

Acts 2:14; Romans 15:13; Galatians 5:5; Ephesians 4:6

The Case: *In what ways does the Holy Spirit change us?*

Simple Supplies: You'll need a Bible, a glue stick, a roll of festive gift wrap, scissors, a marker, and white and yellow construction paper. If you plan on doing the extra-time activity, you'll need additional wrapping paper, scissors, glue, markers, and construction paper.

Before class, prepare and practice this awesome sleight-of-hand trick—kids will love it! First, you'll need to prepare a changing sack that is really two sacks glued together to look like one sack. To make the changing sack, cut two 10-by-14-inch rectangles of wrapping paper. (Try to cut the exact pattern for each rectangle.) Fold the first rectangle in the center and glue the sides to make a sack. Do the same for the second rectangle, making sure the sacks match in the direction of any pattern on the paper. Now glue the sacks together back to back, first turning one bag upside down. Cut two 3-by-5-inch construction rectangles, one white and one yellow. On the yellow one write: "Changed to be ready, willing, and able through the Spirit!" Slide the yellow card into one of the sacks. During the object talk, you'll write words on the white card, then place it in the empty sack. (The other sack contains the yellow card and is facing downward, so you'll have to hold this sack slyly closed!) At the appointed time, you'll secretly turn the sack upside down, and the yellow card will now be in the sack that's facing up! Neat, isn't it? (Hint: Keep whatever sack is face down pinched together to keep the card

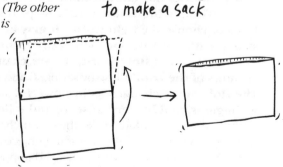

Glue two sides together to make a sack

from falling out!) If there's time, kids will be making their own changing sacks to use at home in presenting this cool object talk to their families and friends.

Discover 'n Do!

Have the yellow card in place, making sure the card is in the sack that faces down. (Pinch the opening closed!) Hold the white card and have a marker close by. Say: **I have blank, white card here. It is nothing special or powerful, but with a little switch-o, change-o it can be! Let's drop this plain card into this amazing changing sack I have and see what happens.** Quickly show kids the inside of the empty sack, then invite a volunteer to drop the card into the empty part of the sack. As you distract kids by talking, slyly turn the sack upside down so the yellow card is now in the upward sack. (Pinch the bottom opening closed.)

Say: **You know, change can be so wonderful when the changes are for good. What do you think has happened to the white card? Will it be changed? Let's find out!** Have another child open the sack and pull out the yellow card and read it aloud. Then say: **Wow! What a change! From an old boring white to yellow and bright! Can we change our thoughts and attitudes this quickly? Can we go from being stubborn to willing, from shy to bold, or from hopeless to hopeful this noticeably? We can when we let the Holy Spirit be the one who changes us! Let's see what we can discover about change with a little detective work and the Bible!**

Collect the Clues!

Say: **When we love and are open to the Holy Spirit, he changes us in powerful ways. The Holy Spirit gives us an attitude of willingness, an attitude of bravery, and an attitude of hope. We become changed in powerful ways for God and become more ready, willing, and able to serve him, obey him, and love him. Let's see what God's Word says about the ways we're changed by the Holy Spirit.** Read aloud these verses: Acts 2:14; 4:8a, 13; Romans 15:13; Galatians 5:5; and Ephesians 4:4. Then ask:

✔ **How does the Holy Spirit help us to be brave? to have courage to tell others about Jesus? to stand on God's Word?**

✔ **In what ways does the Spirit change us from hopeless to having heaps of hope?**

✔ **How does our faith become changed through the Holy Spirit?**

Say: **Without the Holy Spirit's help, it's often hard to tell others about Jesus or choose the right words. It may be tough to hold on to hope or keep strong faith. And we may shy away from serving God and others. But by the power of the Holy Spirit, we are changed into ready, willing, and able servants of the Lord!** Close by saying: **Good for you—you've solved the clues! The Holy Spirit changes us in powerful ways by giving us a spirit of hope, willingness, and bravery to serve and follow God. The case is closed!**

If there's time, let kids make their own changing sacks and cards to take home. Challenge kids to share this awesome object talk with their families and friends as they remind others how we are changed in powerful ways through the Holy Spirit.

T OTAL TRUTH

Luke 12:12; John 16:13; 1 Corinthians 2:9-14; 1 John 5:6

The Case: *Is it possible for the Holy Spirit to lie to us?*

Simple Supplies: You'll need a Bible and two large safety pins. If you plan on doing the extra-time activity, you'll also need scissors, several bags of small and medium-sized safety pins, and craft felt.

Before class, practice this neat trick with safety pins. You'll be hooking two safety pins together then amazingly release them in one swift movement to illustrate how the Holy Spirit untangles lies and gives us the truth. Link the safety pins together. To release the pins, simply hold the base of one pin in your left hand and the head of the second pin in your right hand. (The upper-most bar of the second pin should be held close to the head of the first pin.) At the appropriate time, pull the pins in a firm, quick downward movement of the right-hand pin. This quick movement actually opens the first pin to release the second pin—but is so quick the audience won't notice and the pins will appear to have melted through one another! Kids will be making neat safety-pin wrist wraps, if there's time.

Discover 'n Do!

Gather kids in front of you and hold the two pins, one in each hand but not linked yet. Ask kids to tell about times they were told a lie or even told one themselves. Encourage kids to express how lies feel when they're told or heard. Then say: **Lies seem to be all around us at times. God knows that lies hurt us and others and also hurt him. That's why God's Word tells us not to lie. In fact, not telling lies is the ninth commandment God gave us long ago. Lies hurt us and hurt God, and even the smallest of fibs can tangle us up until we're stuck in big lies!** Fasten the pins together and try to pull them apart to show kids how they're linked together. Then have a child try to pull apart the pins. Continue: **Lies tangle us up, but there is someone who can never lie and, in fact, releases us from lies to help us discover the truth!** Swiftly release the pins with your quick, downward motion, then hold up the separated pins. **The Holy Spirit helps us separate the lies from the truth every time! But why is the truth so important to the Spirit, and how does he help us be truthful? Let's see if we can solve this case with a little detective work and the Bible!**

Collect the Clues!

Form four groups: one Who group, one What group, and two How groups. Then assign each group a verse as follows: 1 John 5:6b (the Who group); John 16:13 (the What group); and Luke 12:12 and 1 Corinthians 2:9-14 (the How groups).

Have the Who group read their verse to discover who is the truth, the What group to discover what the Spirit will do to help us find the truth, and the How group to discover how the Spirit helps us be truthful. After groups have read and discussed their verses, have them share with the entire class their discoveries. Then ask:

✔ **How does seeking the truth instead of settling for lies show our respect for God?**

✔ **How are truth and the words we say related? How are our actions related to what is true?**

✔ **Why is it important to tell truth from lies?**

✔ **In what ways do lies keep us tied to more lies?**

Read aloud John 8:32, then ask:

✔ **What does God's Word mean when it says, "the truth will set you free"?**

Say: **God's Word warns us of many lies and much deceit. Without the help of the Holy Spirit in discerning truth from lies, we can be led astray and believe things about faith and God that may not be true. It's nice to know that if you ever have doubts about what you see or hear or are being taught, you can ask the help of the Holy Spirit to separate lies from truth.** Close by saying: **Good for you—you've solved the clues! Is it possible for the Holy Spirit to ever lie? Of course not! The Holy Spirit always will help us see the truth because the Spirit of God is all truth! This case is closed!**

If there's time, kids will like making cool Truth Wrist Wraps to remind them how the Holy Spirit is the Spirit of truth and will guide us in all truth. For each wrist wrap, cut a 2-inch-wide strip of craft felt a bit larger than the circumference of your wrist. Fasten safety pins in patterns vertically around the felt, then place the wrist wrap around your wrist and fasten it using another safety pin clipped horizontally.

SPIRIT-POWERED!

John 3:34; 4:24; 1 Corinthians 2:14; 12:4, 5; Hebrews 9:14

The Case: *What does it mean to be "empowered"?*

Simple Supplies: You'll need a Bible, a clear plastic cup, a pitcher of water, two 6-inch squares of cheesecloth, a paper plate, a sheet of paper, tape, a marker, and a rubber band. If you plan on doing the extra-time activity, you'll need scissors, white self-adhesive paper, and colorful permanent markers.

Before class, practice this clever object talk to become familiar with how it works. Fill a clear plastic cup with water, then lay the two squares of cheesecloth over the top. Secure the cheesecloth using a rubber band. Wet the entire surface of the cheesecloth covering the top of the cup with your wet hand. Now quickly turn the cup upside down on the paper plate. (A bit of water may escape, but it will stop immediately.) Lift the cup from the plate (keep it upside down) and gently push on

the cheesecloth with your finger. Bubbles will rise to the top of the cup, giving the appearance of boiling water! When the bubbles stop, set the cup on the paper plate right-side up. (Dry out the cheesecloth before performing this object talk.) Tape a sheet of paper to the wall and have a marker handy. If there's time, kids will be making bumper stickers for their bikes, backpacks, or notebooks.

Discover 'n Do!

Be sure you've taped a sheet of paper to a wall or door and have a marker ready. Place the cup, pitcher of water, rubber band, cheesecloth squares, and paper plate on a table. Gather kids around the table, hold up the cup, and say: **Let's pretend this cup is who we are. We're like empty vessels for God, ready to be used in powerful ways. But first, two things must happen: We must be filled, then powered up to get going for God! The Holy Spirit does both of these things for us.** Invite a child to fill the cup three-fourths full of water from the pitcher as you say: **First, the Holy Spirit fills us with fuel to get us going. This fuel includes God's Word, hope, faith, truth, wisdom, and a willing spirit. Next, he covers us with his love and guidance and prepares us to go for God.** Cover the cup with the cheesecloth and secure it with the rubber band. Wet the top of the cheesecloth with your wet hand, then quickly turn the cup upside down on the paper plate. **Then, finally, the Holy Spirit gives us the "go power" we need to get us serving God. With his perfect and powerful touch** (have a child gently push on the cheesecloth as you slightly push downward holding the cup), **we bubble over with joy and willingness to serve God in amazing ways! In other words, the Holy Spirit "empowers" us to serve God. But what exactly does "empowering us" mean, and how does the Spirit help empower us to serve God? Let's see if we can solve this case with a little detective work and the Bible!** Set the cup right-side up on the paper plate.

Collect the Clues!

Gather kids by the paper on the wall and number the paper vertically one to three. Tell kids there are three main things the Holy Spirit empowers or enables us to do. Then read the following sets of verses and have kids identify what the Spirit empowers us to do, which are listed in parentheses beside the verses.

- ✔ ***John 3:34 and 1 Corinthians 2:14*** (The Spirit empowers us to learn God's Word and understand Scripture.)
- ✔ ***1 Corinthians 12:4, 5 and Hebrews 9:14*** (The Spirit empowers us to serve God and others.)
- ✔ ***Luke 1:67-79 and John 4:24*** (The Spirit empowers us to praise and worship God.)

35

After reading and listing the things the Holy Spirit empowers us to do, say: **Wow! The Holy Spirit powers us up to do many things for God. He empowers us to learn and use Scripture, he empowers us to serve God and others, and he empowers us to praise and worship God in loving ways. Without the enabling power of the Holy Spirit, we would be like the cup before our talk—empty.** Ask:

✔ **Why do you think the Holy Spirit wants us to "go for God"?**

✔ **In what ways does having a spirit of willingness help us serve God and others? learn God's Word? worship God?**

Say: **The word** *empowered* **means having the power to do something. When the Holy Spirit empowers us, he gives us the will and the way to accomplish great things for God. Without the empowerment of the Holy Spirit, we would be empty, useless vessels. But with the vroom-zoom of the Spirit, we're transformed into empowered vessels who can serve God and others in wondrous ways!** Close by saying: **Good for you—you've solved the clues! Empowered means having the go-power to serve God. And our go-power comes from the Holy Spirit. This case is closed!**

If there's time, kids will enjoy making Go-Power bumper stickers to place on their bikes, backpacks, or notebooks as reminders that only the Holy Spirit empowers us to get up and go for God. Cut 12-by-4-inch rectangles from self-adhesive white paper. Use permanent markers to write "Powered by the Holy Spirit" or some other power-ful slogan on the bumper stickers. Then finish coloring or decorating the stickers any way you wish. (Tell kids not to place the stickers on their parents' cars unless they first ask permission!)

OUTTA THE BLUE

Romans 15:13; Galatians 5:5; Ephesians 4:3

The Case: *How does the Holy Spirit bring us peace?*

Simple Supplies: You'll need a Bible and a men's handkerchief. If you plan on doing the extra-time activity, you'll need colorful permanent markers and a men's handker-chief for each person.

Before class, practice this simple illusion using a men's handkerchief. (Make sure the handkerchief is soft and not stiff, new cotton. Crinkle and uncrinkle the handkerchief several times to soften the cotton.) Tie a small knot in one corner of the handkerchief. Hold the handkerchief in your right hand by the knotted corner so that the knot is slyly hidden in your hand. Point to the bottom corner, then lift it with your left hand and place that corner in your right hand. Shake the hanky several times and at the same time let go of the knotted corner while keeping hold of the other end. It will seem as if this knot just appeared "outta the blue"! If there's

time, kids will enjoy making a special object-talk handkerchief and learning the trick behind the illusion to perform at home for family and friends.

Discover 'n Do!

Have the handkerchief in your right hand with the knot already hidden in your hand. Gather kids in front of you and ask them to tell about times they were very worried. Encourage kids to tell how their worries finally went away and how they were brought peace of mind. Then hold the handkerchief and say: **There are times when we all worry and long for peace of heart and mind. Some solutions to worry just mask our problems** (hold the hanky over your face for a moment), **or they just cover over our worries** (drape the hanky, still holding the concealed knot, over a child's head). **But still we can't find the peace we need or the hope to hang on to. Even a knot of hope would help! It's at these times, when we feel at the end of our rope** (lift the far corner and place it in your hand), **that we must trust the power of the Holy Spirit to send us help and hope** (shake the hanky and let the knot come tumbling down) **outta the blue! Wow! The Holy Spirit can bring us peace and hope to hang on to! But how does the Spirit bring us peace and hope, and why is having inner peace so important? Let's see if we can solve this case with a little detective work and the Bible!**

Collect the Clues!

Invite kids to read aloud the following verses about peace, hope, and the Holy Spirit: Romans 15:13; Galatians 5:5; and Ephesians 4:3. Then ask:

✔ **How does finding hope help us have peace of heart and mind?**
✔ **In what ways does trusting the Holy Spirit and his power bring us peace? give us hope to hang on to?**
✔ **How does having peace of mind and heart draw us closer to God? help us praise and honor him more?**

Say: **Worries keep us from having the inner peace it takes to rely on God or to serve him with all our hearts. When so much room in our hearts is taken up with worry, there's not enough room to love God fully. That's why the Holy Spirit wants to bring us God's peace, hope, and serenity to hold on to.**

Close by saying: **Good for you—you've solved the clues! The Holy Spirit brings us hope and peace to rid us of the worries that keep us from loving and serving God with all our hearts. This case is closed!**

If there's time, invite kids to make their own handkerchief props. Use colorful permanent markers to write Romans 15:13 on the handkerchiefs, then show kids how to perform this cool illusion. Challenge kids to give this powerful object talk to their families and friends as reminders of how the Holy Spirit brings us peace, hope, and lots of love to hang on to!

FILLED TO FOCUS

Psalms 29:2; 100:1, 2; Luke 4:8; John 4:23, 24

The Case: *How does the Holy Spirit help us worship God?*

Simple Supplies: You'll need a Bible, a clear glass, a pitcher of water, and a cork. If you plan on doing the extra-time craft activity, you'll also need dried potpourri and cloves, foam-board hearts, ribbon, scissors, and tacky craft glue.

Before class, practice this clever object-talk trick to become familiar with how it works. Pour water into a glass and fill it to about 3-inches from the top. Place a cork in the center of the glass. It won't stay in the center until you fill the glass with as much water as it can possibly hold. Then the cork will gravitate to the center. You'll use this demonstration to show kids that only when we are filled with the Holy Spirit can we truly keep God at the center of our worship and lives. After the object talk, kids will be making potpourri hearts as reminders that the scent of sweet worship rises to God's heart as the scent of sweet incense rises upward. Use a utility-type knife to cut 6-inch foam-board hearts before class.

Discover 'n Do!

Set the clear glass, pitcher of water, and cork on a table. Fill the cup with water to within 3-inches of the rim. Then gather kids around the table and challenge a volunteer to place the cork in the center of the water.

When the child tries repeatedly and fails, say: **Keeping this cork in the center of the water is like trying to keep God as the center of our worship when we don't have the Holy Spirit in our lives. We become distracted. We may not worship with a sincere heart or mind. And perhaps we only give God a small portion of the praise and honor due him. But God wants all of our hearts and minds and sincerity when we come before him in worship, so how do we keep God at the center? We fill ourselves to the brim with the Holy Spirit!**

Pour water into the glass and fill it completely. When the cork moves to the center, say: **When we're filled with the Spirit, we can keep God at the center of our worship and our lives as well. But how does the Holy Spirit help us worship God, and why is it important to worship in the Spirit? Let's see if we can solve the case with a little detective work and the Bible!**

Collect the Clues!

Read aloud Luke 4:8; Psalms 29:2; 100:1, 2; and John 4:23, 24. Then ask:

✔ Why are we to worship only God and no one else?
✔ Why do you think God wants our sincerest love when we worship him?
✔ What does it mean to worship in "spirit and in truth"?

✔ **In what ways does the Holy Spirit help us worship in truth? help us worship with a sincere heart and mind? help us express ourselves in worship?**

Say: **Keeping God at the center of our worship allows us to focus on God and who he is so we can praise him for what he does. Being filled with the Holy Spirit helps us worship and honor God with all our love. But when we have the Holy Spirit filling our lives, God isn't just at the center of our worship—he is at the center of our lives, too!** Close by saying: **Good for you— you've solved the clues! The Holy Spirit helps us keep God at the center of our worship and of our lives. And the Spirit guides us in worshiping in spirit and in truth, just as God wants us to worship. The case is closed!**

If there's time, let kids make aromatic incense hearts to remind them that worship rises to God as a sweet scent of the heart. For each heart, spread tacky craft glue over a heart shape made from foam board. Sprinkle dried potpourri and cloves on the glue. Finally, glue a 6-inch ribbon loop to the top of the heart for hanging. Let the glue dry thoroughly before hanging in a closet, window, or room.

ESCAPE HATCH

Romans 8:1-14; Ephesians 3:16

The Case: *In what ways does the Holy Spirit set us free?*

Simple Supplies: You'll need a Bible, three small silk scarves or pieces of silk (different colors), a 10-inch piece of white thread, a clear glass tumbler, and a rubber band. If you plan on doing the extra-time activity, you'll need one of the silk squares from the object talk.

Before class, prepare and practice this awesome object talk to become smooth in your presentation. Tie the thread to one corner of the silk that will be the "escaping" silk, then tie a small knot at the other end of the thread. During the object talk, you'll place the escaping silk in the bottom of the clear glass tumbler but slyly make sure that the thread is hanging outside the glass. Place a silk of different color on top of the first one in the glass, then cover the glass with the third square of silk and hold it in place around the top of the glass using a rubber band. (Make sure the rubber band isn't too tight so the escaping silk can slide out later.) At the appropriate time, you'll reach beneath the silk cover to find the knotted thread. Pull the thread quickly, and the escaping silk will quickly slide out of the glass so it seems to be escaping on it's own! (Don't let kids see the thread!) After the object talk, kids will enjoy a lively game of Escape Hatch. (Hint: For this trick, use very thin silk material and thread as well as a semi-loose rubber band to aid in the slippery escape!)

Discover 'n Do!

Place the glass tumbler, rubber band, and squares of silk on a table. (Keep track of where the hidden thread is on your escaping silk!) Say: **The Bible often talks of people being slaves to their natures. This means that people tend to do only what makes them feel good or is fun, not necessarily good for them. For example, if you could eat brownies or spinach, which would you choose?** Allow kids to respond, then continue: **Or if you could have the afternoon to play with your friends or study, which would you choose? People naturally want to take the easy road or the feel-good path, and that can leave us slaves or prisoners to bad habits and unhealthy living. It can even lead us away from God. In other words, we become trapped!** Place the escaping silk at the bottom of the glass, then place the other silk on top and cover the glass with the third silk and rubber band.

Say: **Just like the silk in the bottom of the glass, we can become trapped by our sinful human nature. We need help! But who can help us escape or set us free? The Holy Spirit can set us free!** Pull the thread to make the silk amazingly escape the glass. Say: **Wow! Free at last! And that is just what the Holy Spirit can do for us when we trust him to guide our living. But how can the Spirit set us free, and how does living a life free of the chains of sin help us draw closer to God? Let's see if we can solve the case with a little detective work and the Bible!**

Collect the Clues!

Form five groups and assign each group one of the following passages from Romans 8 to read: Romans 8:1, 2; 8:5, 6; 8:7-9; 8:11; and 8:14. Have groups read the verses and discuss what is being taught about the Holy Spirit and how we are set free to live through the Spirit. Then have groups read their verses, in order, and share their discoveries with the entire class. Ask:

- ✔ **In what ways does our being weak humans destroy us if we just do what we want to and live carelessly?**
- ✔ **What changes in our lives when we live according to the Spirit and not according to our earthly wants?**
- ✔ **How can living a life led by our own wants keep us prisoners living away from God?**
- ✔ **How can living according to God's Spirit lead us closer to God?**

Read aloud Ephesians 3:16 and Romans 8:14 once more. Then say: **When we love the Holy Spirit and ask him to guide us, we are led by the Spirit and are called sons of God. That's an awesome truth to think about, isn't it? We are set free, are led by the Holy Spirit, and are sons of God!** Close by saying: **Good for you—you've solved the clues! The Holy Spirit sets us free from sin and eternal death through guiding us away from our sinful natures and leading us toward God. The case is closed!**

 **40**

If there's time, play a lively game of Escape Hatch. Have kids form a circle, then choose one child to stand in the center of the circle and another child to stand outside of the circle. Hand the child inside the circle one of the silk squares from the object talk and explain that the object of the game is to help the silk scarf escape the circle by passing, tossing, or sliding the scarf to the player outside the circle. Players in the circle can only block with one of their arms and must hold their others arms to their sides. When a pass is completed, have the two children choose two others to provide an escape hatch for the scarf.

TEAM SPIRIT!

John 14:16, 17; Romans 8:26-28; Philippians 2:1, 2

The Case: *How can we work with the Holy Spirit as a team?*

Simple Supplies: You'll need a Bible. If you plan on doing the extra-time activity, you'll also need tacky craft glue, scissors, glitter, craft felt scraps, and a square of colorful craft felt for each child.

Before class, practice this simple trick with a couple of family members to get the hang of how it works. Here's the setup: While one person (your secret partner) is out of the room, the others choose an item that everyone can see, such as a flower vase. When the person returns to the room, you begin asking questions such as, "Is it the clock?" or "Is it the bookshelf?" Suddenly your partner knows it is the flower vase and shouts, "Yes!" How did he know? Before the stunt, you both chose the letter "B" (as in bookshelf). Right after you asked if it was an object beginning with the letter B, you asked about the item chosen by the group. Simple, isn't it? But your audience will be very amazed and baffled! After the object talk, kids will enjoy making their own Team Spirit pennants from colorful felt.

Discover 'n Do!

Before class, pull a child aside and secretly clue him in to the trick you'll perform during object talk time. Be sure you both understand which letter has been chosen as a cue. (Using the letter "B" works well, since Bible, book, bookshelf, and backpack all begin with the letter B and leave room to do the trick two or three times if you're asked for an encore!)

Gather kids and ask them what their favorite sports teams are. Then say: **Teamwork can be lots of fun. Let's see how a bit of teamwork works right now. I'll choose someone to leave the class for a moment while the rest of us choose an item in plain view in the room. Then when our absent person returns, I'll ask questions, and we'll see if he can guess the object you all chose. Now who would like to leave the room for a moment?** Pretend to have

a hard decision, then choose your secret partner to leave the room. When the rest of the kids have chosen an item in plain sight, call your partner back into the room. Ask your questions until you name an item beginning with the letter B. When the next item is named, your partner should shout, "Yes!" Kids will be surprised and may ask to repeat the trick, but say: **That was fun, and you all worked well as a team. I had a partner in this trick, too!** Introduce your partner and have him explain how the trick was done. Then say: **We can accomplish lots of things through teamwork and cooperation and communication. And that's just what the Holy Spirit wants us to realize: that we're partners with him. But what does it mean to be in partnership with the Holy Spirit, and how does being a partner with the Spirit help make our faith stronger? Let's see if we can solve the case with a little detective work and the Bible!**

Collect the Clues!

Read aloud the following verses about being in partnership with the Holy Spirit: Romans 8:26-28; Philippians 2:1, 2; John 14:16, 17; and 2 Corinthians 13:14. Then ask:

✔ **What does it mean to be "like-minded"?**

✔ **How can being a partner with the Holy Spirit draw us closer to God?**

Say: **The Holy Spirit knows that God gave us free will and choice, and the Spirit doesn't bully us into following him. The Holy Spirit wants us to follow him and be led by him of our own free choice. In other words, the Spirit of God doesn't want to be our boss and bully us; he wants to be our friend, counselor, guide, and partner!** Ask:

✔ **What can we accomplish if we choose to have the Holy Spirit as our partner?**

Say: **Without my partner earlier, we couldn't have done the fun trick we did. And without the Holy Spirit as our spiritual partner, we can't accomplish God's will in our lives. God's Word tells us that all things work for good when we're called according to God's purpose. The Holy Spirit knows God's thoughts and will and can lead us in accomplishing all God wants us to accomplish. Being a part of the Holy Spirit's team puts us on the best team in the whole world.** Close by saying: **Good for you—you've solved the clues! Being partners with the Holy Spirit means he will guide us if we choose to follow him in accomplishing God's will in our lives. The case is closed!**

If there's time, let kids design and make Team Spirit pennants to hang in their rooms as reminders of the importance of being partners with the Holy Spirit. Help kids cut out pennant-shapes from their craft felt. Glue on snazzy felt logos or patterns representing the Holy Spirit, such as doves, hearts, lightning bolts, or power blasts. Then add glitter letters to spell out "I have team SPIRIT" on the pennants for a sparkly effect.

OLLOW THE LEADER

Ezekiel 36:27, 28; Romans 8:14; Ephesians 1:17

The Case: *How does the Holy Spirit lead us to God?*

Simple Supplies: You'll need a Bible, two nickels and a dime, a clear plastic cup, and a table covered with a tablecloth. If you plan on doing the extra-time activity, you'll also need paper plates.

Before class, practice setting up and performing this neat object talk. Be sure you have a table covered with a tablecloth. Place the three coins in a row with the dime in the center. Place a clear plastic cup or glass upside down so that its rim sits on the two nickels. During the object talk, you'll challenge kids to think of a way to remove the coin from beneath the cup without touching any of the coins or the cup. At the appropriate time, begin scratching the cloth in front of the cup. Keep scratching and the dime will slowly "walk" out from under the cup all by itself! (Slick, isn't it?) After the object talk, kids will do a lively relay about following the leader.

Discover 'n Do!

Place the coins and cup on the tablecloth in the setup position, with the dime under the cup and the cup sitting on the nickels. Ask kids if they've ever felt trapped in a tough situation or thought there was no way out of a problem they had. Encourage kids to tell how it felt to be trapped, frustrated, and maybe even hopeless. Then say: **This was much how God's people felt when they were trapped after fleeing Egypt. Let's pretend this dime is how we feel when we're trapped by trouble. In the case of God's people long ago, they were trapped with evil Pharaoh on one side of them and the mighty Red Sea on the other. What were they told to do? God told Moses to follow him, and he would show them the path to freedom. What happened in the story?**

As kids briefly retell the story of how God parted the Red Sea, begin scratching the cloth in front of the cup and continue until the dime has walked to freedom. Then say: **Yea! Moses and the Israelites followed God's directions and were led out of the trap and into freedom in an amazing way! God helped many people throughout the pages of the Bible escape traps and evil, and he led them into freedom. Listen to what God promised Ezekiel about how God would move him.**

Read aloud Ezekiel 36:27, then say: **God promised to put his Spirit into Ezekiel to lead him in obedience and in following God. The Holy Spirit was**

hard at work so long ago, and he still is today! The Holy Spirit is here to guide us to freedom and lead us closer to God. But how does the Holy Spirit lead us closer to God? Let's see if we can solve the case with a little detective work and the Bible!

Collect the Clues!

Invite kids to read aloud the following verses as they discover more about how the Holy Spirit leads and guides us closer to God: Ezekiel 36:27, 28; John 16:13; Ephesians 1:17; and 1 John 3:24. Then ask:

✔ **How does the Spirit help us follow God's commands and rules?**
✔ **In what way does being obedient to God and following the Spirit draw us closer to God? strengthen our faith?**
✔ **What happens if we choose to follow someone or something else instead of God's Spirit?**
✔ **How can we find help and freedom by being led by the Holy Spirit?**

Read aloud Romans 8:14, then say: **When we are led by the Holy Spirit, not only do we understand and obey God's commands more—we are called his children! The Holy Spirit is truly the leader we want to follow each day of our lives.** Close by saying: **Good for you—you've solved the clues! The Holy Spirit leads us closer to God by showing us how to obey God better, giving us freedom to follow God, and helping us become children of God. The case is closed!**

If there's time, form three or four small groups and have them line up at one end of the classroom. The first person in each line is the leader. Hand each player two paper plates. Explain that in this follow-the-leader type game, all players must travel the same path as the leader in their line chooses but cannot step on the floor—only on paper plates used as steppingstones! Place one plate down and step on it before placing the next plate on the floor. Any time you call "switch," the leaders go to the backs of the lines and the next players in line become the new leaders. Continue around the room in this fashion until everyone has been the leader at least once.

GOOD OUTTA BAD

1 Corinthians 1:18; 2:12, 13; 1 Thessalonians 1:6

The Case: *How does the Holy Spirit help us have positive attitudes?*

Simple Supplies: You'll need a Bible, newspapers, scissors, white paper, clear tape, a marker, and red-construction paper. If you plan on doing the extra-time activity, you'll need vanilla, peanut butter, powdered sugar, rolled oats, self-sealing sandwich bags, plastic spoons, and raisins.

Before class, prepare the newspaper with the secret pocket to use in the object talk. Take a sheet of newspaper and place it on a table. Take a second sheet of newspaper and cut a 4-by-3-inch rectangle from the left-hand side about halfway down the paper. Tape or glue the rectangle to the matching side of the first sheet of newspaper. (The rectangle should very closely match the original paper, just have different story printing but retain the left-hand margin space.) From a distance, your audience should not be able to tell that there is a secret pocket in the sheet of newspaper. Now cut a 5-inch red paper heart, fold it a couple of times, and smooth it very flat. Slide the heart into the secret pocket. During the object talk, you'll hold the sheet of newspaper and turn it back and forth quickly as if you're reading the news. Keep your left or right hand covering the pocket so the heart doesn't fall out. Then at the appropriate time, you'll tear up the paper (saving the pocket for last) and at the last moment quickly pull the paper heart from the hidden pocket as if the heart appeared from nowhere out of the paper! (Very neat and puzzling for kids!) After the object talk, kids will like making bitter vanilla into a sweet treat as a tasty reminder that the Holy Spirit helps us find goodness in the face of bitterness. Finally, tape a sheet of paper to the wall or door and have a marker handy.

Discover 'n Do!

Hold the newspaper with the hidden pocket. (Be sure the heart is in place and keep hold of that side of the paper.) Pretend to read the paper or even read part of an article about something negative such as a robbery or a fight. Then say: **Wow. It seems that our newspapers are filled every day with negative things and stories that are sad.** (Turn the paper around several times as you talk so kids can see there's nothing stuck to the paper.) Continue: **Stories about wars and robberies, fighting, and killing—sometimes I begin to wonder how anyone can stay happy and positive in the face of all the negatives of our world. Do you feel that way, too? It makes me angry to read all of this!**

Tear up the paper (saving the pocket) and, at the last moment, quickly and slyly pull out the paper heart and hold it up in surprise. Say: **Oh my! Where did this heart come from? Could there have been love and kindness in the midst of so much meanness and fighting? Yes! Love is always there if we take the time to look and guard against having a hard, cold heart from all the negatives we encounter. But we need help to keep softened hearts and love, and the Holy Spirit is the one to help us! Just how does the Holy Spirit help us see love through hate and sunshine through storms? Let's see if we can solve the case with a little detective work and the Bible!**

Collect the Clues!

Gather kids by the paper you taped to the wall or door. Divide the paper in half and place a negative sign (-) at the top of one half and a positive sign (+) at the top of the other half. Explain that you'll read verses and decide what negative hearts see and what positive hearts see in the verse and list them on the paper. Read the following verses and follow the suggestions for the negatives and positives given in parentheses beside the reference.

45

✔ *1 Corinthians 1:18* (Negative hearts see Jesus' death as foolish; positive hearts see his death as life and forgiveness.)

✔ *1 Corinthians 2:12, 13* (Negative hearts see the spirit of the world and sin; positive hearts see the Spirit of God.)

✔ *1 Thessalonians 1:6* (Negative hearts see suffering; positive hearts see joy.)

Say: **When we see negative things and people and have a hardened heart or an "I-don't-care" attitude, we become cynical and pessimistic. And we fail to see the goodness, love, and blessings God puts all around us.** Read aloud 2 Corinthians 13:14, then continue: **Having a hard heart toward God and others is an awful thing to have! That's why the Holy Spirit softens our hearts to feel kindness and love in the face of meanness and hate. And the Spirit helps us see the good things and blessings God brings even when bad and evil are all around us.** Ask:

✔ **How does a negative attitude keep us from loving God? from loving others?**

✔ **What is the good of having a warm heart and caring attitude even when there are negative situations or people around us?**

Say: **I'm so glad the Holy Spirit helps us keep a loving heart and positive attitude even in the face of negatives, aren't you? That way I can see God's blessings and praise him for every one of them!** Close by saying: **Good for you—you've solved the clues! The Holy Spirit allows us to see the good through the bad and to have loving, caring attitudes that help us recognize God's blessings. This case is closed!**

If there's time, hand each child a self-sealing sandwich bag containing a plastic spoonful of vanilla. Have kids try a taste of plain vanilla on their tongues. Encourage kids to express how it tastes and tell them that this taste represents what a bitter heart feels like. Then add the following to each bag: a spoonful of peanut butter, two spoons of powdered sugar, a spoon of rolled oats, and a spoon of raisins. Mix the ingredients in the bags, then taste the result. Have kids tell how the negative, bitter taste turned to sweetness. Remind kids that the power of the Spirit helps us turn bitterness to sweetness and negatives to positives.

ETERNAL SPIRIT

John 3:34; 14:16; Hebrews 9:14

The Case: *How long will the Holy Spirit be with us?*

Simple Supplies: You'll need a Bible, a small cloth or vinyl zippered coin purse, a gift bow, a 24-inch dowel rod (¼-inch diameter), and scissors. If you plan on doing the extra-time activity, you'll also need a bow, small coin purse, and 12-inch dowel rod for each child.

Before class, prepare and practice this eye-popping stunt to become smooth in your presentation. This is an incredible illusion, and your kids will go wild for it! First, obtain a small, palm-sized cloth or vinyl zippered coin purse—one you can easily snip a hole in. Snip a hole in the edge opposite the zippered side. Make the hole just shy of ½-inch or slightly larger than the thin dowel rod you have. Stick a bow to the top of the coin purse. (You'll need to wear long sleeves for this cool trick.) Slide the dowel rod through the zippered opening in the coin purse and up your sleeve, leaving about one inch of rod in the purse. Zip the coin purse closed and hold the purse in your palm with your thumb on the top of it to give it support and keep it from slipping off your hand. (This will destroy the presentation!) Obviously, when kids see the small purse on your palm, they will not imagine something 2-foot long could be hiding inside—especially a 2-foot-long wooden rod! At the appointed time, carefully unzip the coin purse and proceed to slowly pull the dowel rod out from the purse opening. Kids will be amazed at this unbelievable feat! If there's time after the object talk, plan on letting kids make their own Eternal Gift coin purses so they can present this awesome object talk at home. (Hint: Make sure your audience sees no gap between the coin purse and your sleeve—you want the dowel rod to remain a secret!)

Discover 'n Do!

Just prior to your talk time, leave the room for a moment and place the dowel rod up your sleeve and position the coin purse with the bow on your palm. Make sure there is about one inch of rod sticking into the purse.

Gather kids in front of you (but not too close!) and say: **I am holding a gift in my hand to represent the gifts we are given in our lives. What was the most special gift you ever received, and why was it so special?** Allow kids time to respond, then say: **Gifts are so nice to receive. But some gifts don't seem to last very long. They're forgotten or maybe outgrown or perhaps they break and are tossed away for something better or newer. The Holy Spirit is a gift that we've been given that is very precious and special. But just how long does the gift of the Holy Spirit last? Let's see if our gift box can give us any clues.**

Carefully unzip the coin purse and slowly begin to pull out the dowel rod. As the dowel rod is slowly extracted, say: **Wow! This just seems to go on and on forever, doesn't it? Well, that's just how long the gift of the Holy Spirit lasts—forever!** When the dowel rod is completely removed, say: **You would never have guessed that such a big item would have fit in such a small gift, would you? But the power and love of the Holy Spirit is even bigger, and this is from someone we can't even see except with our hearts and faith! How can we know and trust** that the Holy Spirit will be with us forever? Let's see if we can solve this case with a little detective work and the Bible!

Collect the Clues!

Read each of the following verses, then ask the accompanying questions.

Read aloud John 3:34, then ask:

✔ **What does "without limit" mean?**

✔ **Who has given us the gift of the Holy Spirit without limit?**

✔ **How did God show his love for us by giving us the gift of the Holy Spirit?**

Read aloud John 14:16, then ask:

✔ **Who did Jesus ask God to send us?**

✔ **How long did Jesus say this Counselor would be with us?**

Read aloud Hebrews 9:14, then ask:

✔ **Who did Jesus offer himself through?**

✔ **What does "eternal Spirit" mean?**

✔ **How does the gift of the Holy Spirit help us serve God and love Jesus more?**

Say: **God's Word makes three things very clear: first, that God gave us the Holy Spirit without limit; second, that Jesus died for our sins and offered himself through the Spirit so we could better serve God with clean hearts; and third, that the Holy Spirit is eternal and will be with us forever. It makes me feel so good to know the Holy Spirit is a friend, helper, and guide whom I can count on and put my trust and faith in!** Close by saying: **Good for you—you've solved the clues! The Holy Spirit is alive and with us from today through forever—helping, guiding, and loving us each step of the way! The case is closed!**

If there's time, invite kids to prepare their own Eternal Gift coin purses and dowel rods. Then show kids how to perform this awesome object talk. Let kids practice giving the object talk with partners, then challenge kids to present this powerful message at home for their families and friends.

CASE CLOSED!